on
the
governing
of
empires

Also by Alasdair Paterson

Poems for Douanier Rousseau
Hieronymous Bosch's picture history
Terra Nova
Alps
Topiary
The Floating World: Selected Poems 1973–1982
Brief Lives

on the governing
of empires

ALASDAIR PATERSON

Shearsman Books
Exeter

Published in the United Kingdom in 2010
by
Shearsman Books Ltd
58 Velwell Road
Exeter EX4 4LD

www.shearsman.com

ISBN 978-1-84861-116-0
First Edition

Acknowledgements
Some of these poems were first published
in the following magazines:
Great Works, Obsessed with pipework, Shadowtrain, Shearsman

Cover design by Alys Paterson.

CONTENTS

My grandfather left me 53 volumes on governing the empire. What an inheritance! So far I have read and destroyed 30, and can state that I am in a fair way to forgetting all he knew. Some day, I hope, my children will thank me.
  —Constantine VIII, Emperor of Byzantium: *Letters*

Once upon a time, in a humdrum suburb you won't have heard of, in a town that won't ring any bells even if you've passed through once or twice, my mother and father did what came naturally and there was I—nothing special either, but clutching with radiant hope the usual birthday present, an obligation to sing the words of one song to the tune of another.
  —'Claudette': *A Spy in the Rose Cabaret*

For my family

on heresy

stars come solitaries first
then a host like
pilgrims no crusaders

this rock that bleached
all day in the sun
still isn't white enough

do you prefer
the desert places or
the cities of the plain
I like best the view
of lights from up here

a breath of rosemary
perfection in the air
but the bridge is the devil's

on optics

reading from the top
it's down there they
broke the glass
burned the books
and their true believers
or reasonably similar
or just different

last lines are
the streets shone
then it was darker

on psyche

underneath all of it

fountains and roses
silk weave and moths
morgues birthing chambers
perfumed kisses dripping
clocks and tortures

under all the names
for the gods and their
mouths that can't be parched
for fear of uncomfortable silences

under all of it
you're into the vast
cisterns built for long siege
dim light on amber surfaces
slime and sleek byzantine carp
pillars from unseen to unseen
and round a corner
to stop you in your tracks
head of great medusa

on verbs

we're picking their language over
like looters with a bolt of cloth
a thing of the finest weave
miraculous in shade and balance
though for purposes of siege warfare
surprisingly sub-optimal

to recap the highlights

we cracked the city
but we kept the shell
we fried the generals
but we hired the bowmen
we strung up the gaolers
but we hung onto the keys
we burned the readers
but we doused the librarians
we liquidated the banks
but we floated the accountants
we plundered the estates
but we planted out the gardeners

priests and philosophers
we kept them too as
a classic arena match-up
the stab of the imperative
the net of the conditional

we have not learned their language yet
we are learning their language now
we shall have learned their language soon
our command will be properly stiff
but our spies will be secretly fluent

our spies are almost fluent now
they have been writing almost secret reports

they report that we have changed the world
they confirm that the world continues to change
they beg to inform us that we are changing with the world

on forestry

the living stand tall
in the graveyard harvests
deconsecration is heavy air
is stripped wood disinfectant

catch your breath before
we go under the perpendiculars
grateful for even these
small bird anthems
rustle of misericord
until a dark door shuts

how many parishes
to the first window filled
with corn glow or shepherds

on reformation

ah sweet woods
it's good
in spring you came
to heal our aching windows
with old glass greens

the fishponds ran wild
when our backs were turned
but today a moorhen
we thought
walked on the water
yes right before our eyes

make a note
so far it's promising

on tragedy

out in the drenched unseen
was where the worst
usually came to the best
colonnades are what you think
but colonnades were just
the metrics and a long
echo till the building failed

by then the gods had shut up shop
slipped the search parties
bought gash papers laid low
reopened in the workshop zone
and there they took their long breaks
in the courtyard of chestnut flambeaux
or under a naked storeroom bulb
pointing the workclothes at
a chorus of death masks
and torsos pockmarked with the years
banging on about an upturn as if

nemesis meantime was no longer
the death of the past no
scarcely to be recognised in her
new uptown solo business set-up
focussed and going for volume
and hell if some customers
missed the personal touch
there was no denying
the groaning indexed shelves
those great marketplace stats

on bells

as in the shell
bursts wave on wave
so the toll of these is earth
and its heavy losses
of woods once unploughed
meadows without sourness
poppies before wire

incoming again to
the same sound crater
what are the chances
composite of lost
domains botched relief
and the tallest of tales
the strike not once
not twice but triple
unlucky lucifer
still if you knows
a better hole go to it

sniping the perimeter
birds of no-man's land
persist with the territorial
a last bit of old soldiering
before their hard sardonic songs
evolve to atrocity stories

on princesses

it's so heavy showroom time
so finger in the briarwood
why not let the in-house
team strain off the quest

delivery can be reliable
bedroom express and fit
in gloss matt bone china
or upholstered subject
to classic purse strings

with statutory indoors and outdoors
expect queen-sized cool next the skin
fully injected gold silk lacquer
against damaged possibilities
value-added is the children's range

if or when lines and shadows
strike through the warranties
sleep easy sleep long in
the dream contours of
perpetual life makeover

no stains no pain
no returns either with
pre-planned all-exclusive
personal dispatch
by royal appointment

in a choice of finish

on fire

lightning shimmy   lucifer scratch   liberated spark   libertine
smoulder

leaf spasm   licked spruce   lemontree squeeze   lilac spurt

lacewing shrivel   lizard stencil   leveret skirl   lark suttee

luminous stable   lantern stairwell library smokehouse
lighthouse steeple

lake sanctuary   larch survivor   lung sfumato   lurking sequel

on stars

moon flat
calm waterhole
unruffled torchlight
herds from the cave
walls rumble past

and here again
the classic problem
with the safe seats
even eye to glass
it's an old cold trail
far away and gone
the predators the dead

on statues

iron man iron boot
iron glove iron knock

then it's another morning
in the frozen forest
iron gates not required
and fewer prisoners waking
by the felled timber
to an iron echo

those who didn't jostle
close enough the fire
last night or chose not to
some are pointing
like our iron hero
but you'd wonder where

as they're stacked till spring

on ballads

ah brother
this is the gloomy wood
where no-one comes to find you
and the trees bend like mourners
and briars coil behind you

a man walks into a wood or is already there or just in his
imagination   it's hard work with fragments   seemingly not
a woodcutter anyway or charcoal-burner or forester or pig-
herd or wild man or brigand or anyone who belongs in a
wood   but a brother   a charged term variously expressing
consanguinity loyalty love jealousy murderous opposition
it's hard work with fragments   a voice of indeterminate age
perhaps not young   a wood of indeterminate composition
perhaps a hunched spur of the ancient caledonian unusually
deserted   briars are a nuisance at best and often gravitate to
tragic graves and fairy-tale sanctions

no hermitage no spring
no words of consolation
a sourness is troubling
the scent of woodbine

lack of shelter or counsel or refreshment   frankly a poor
showing for ballad country   consolation where it makes a
rare appearance in such settings never murmurs anyway but
likes to perform in dumb-show   honeysuckle and decay
you say autumn   I say unpropitious

ah brother
your body wasted
and your grey face like mine

confrontation or memory   and questions   like who spoke
just then   how late is it   what fragments of light   the path
where

on midlife

the verandah of your dreams
but how about the perimeter
the shapes in the half-dark
friend or foe

father passed through here
muttering crisis what crisis
became that man we remember
back to the bright lights
face to the sandflies
then came the great leap forward

my take on this
sons and daughter
is that the structure's
at best semi-stable
but light floods in
as well as out
so take as a given
termite energy ghost rot and
try to find time for the skyrockets

on taxonomy

remember
let the dishes come
in their proper order

bring on the silent
unsung vegetable world
to make the board groan
with a kinsman's grace
trumpet in the finny tribe
so distant from their music
and sweet birds tumbled
from the air like myths
we cherished until yesterday
ransack crammed bestiaries
of open ground and forest
meek and proud piled
cheek by jowl and
let them all be suitably
disposed undressed spiced
sauced with mortality

now
unleash the forked animal

on protocol

new men go at luxury pell-mell
but old money likes its napkins

*

if your neighbour takes a second
helping from your portion
be sure to give his daughter
a red face in the morning

*

the older the family
the paler the food-taster

*

contrary to popular belief
a wedding and a funeral
may share floral tributes
and a roast or two

the rest is forensics

*

greet from afar
the emergency back-up food-taster

*

tonight when your allotted place
is unexpectedly far below the salt
glance round

someone will be smiling

*

never eat immoderately of mushrooms
for
as the cook said
to the food-taster
frankly
any dish of woodland fungi
is just accident
or design
waiting to happen

the rest is toxicology

on leadership

this is the right turning
this is the wrong turning
this is my

face both sides of the coin
footprint both ends of the track
hilltop statue worth the scramble
campaign plan worth the stone inscription

a pause here while you read
terrain rain strength march torch
yes didn't it work like a charm

my difference is always
the secret star chart
rolled up in the knapsack

my edge is always
the secret default
rolled up in the charter

which is this is the right
which is this is the wrong
which is
this is
just because

on palaces

house of fame
   shadows flickers

house of pain
   that noble family

house of silence
   hushed were the streets

house of sleep
   stumbling over riddles

house of wax
   the tapers were all out

house of tears
   past the crocodile pond

house of horrors
   you opened the sealed door

house of oedipus

on monasteries

here
in between
and for a limited season
as records show
the cells grew luminous
ink flowed and dried

there was lucid depth
with squalls
music of the spheres
and shells
latin glossed
with gull cries

beachcombers
now where are
your marks
along the tideline
your stone on stone

spilled rosaries
from the air
past telling

foreword
and afterword
the rock
the sand
the sea

on bedlam

presenting for your edification

the dark spectacle   the merveille du jour

as we unlock the doors to

the suspected   the uncertain   the anomalous

herein presented as

*the dingy footman   the sallow kitten   the coxscomb prominent
the ruddy highflier   the mottled beauty   the lead-coloured drab
the chinese character   the feathered gothic   the powdered quaker
the autumnal rustic   the apple-leaf skeletoniser*

to chill the blood with strange tales of

*the satin lutestring   the bulrush wainscot   the toadflax brocade
the buttoned snout   the flame shoulder   the blotched emerald   the
clouded silver   the lunar thorn   the glaucous shears   the rest
harrow   the ghost swift*

concluding with a modest presentation of my own area

the black arches   the old lady   the skin moth

on memory

clumps of stones and timber fragments visible at low tide
as I went down to the harbour wall
as I climbed into the bottomless boat
I looked back and back but no tears came

a fragment of weft-faced compound twill or samite
what was the perfume it carried
the cloth she used to staunch the blood
before my wound caught cold

a mound and contours of a moat
morning light shone through a casement
the lips I think were similar
it was maybe her name but no not the face

place names confirm a once-extensive afforestation
where does madness take you
I was sleeping out in the wildwood
so pitiful my enemy spared me

a blade with flat thin cross-section and vestigial inscription
we kept this sword between us as we slept
it read defensor fidei
it corroded

the lower section of a blue glass bottle with indeterminate residue
we like our stories with endings and beginnings
and of course the love potion
I had quite forgotten the love potion

on the senses

little saints buried saints
finally kissed by the earth
lilies from your parched mouths
from your salt lips
rise white and tall
scented but with which world

tonight your funeral mass
is being chanted again
in the drowned city
its incense fills us
spume and lightning

on salvage

there it was indelibly
on my arm
I love you jo
except I didn't
any more

my friends said laser
the 21st century eraser
but that risk of scarring
then how would I ever forget
so with my closure consultant
I planned instead the minimal
intervention arm re-edit

we got started with
I loved you jo
a moment of closure yes
but surely a lifetime's rehash
ensuing

then
I love your jodhpurs
quite a good stab if
cryptic in certain situations
except I'm a city boy
and I hate that horse-sweat

I'd love your job
bit of a false trail there
confrontational
and let's be honest
probably I wouldn't

Is love your journey
utterly fluttery
scattergun of fey
and never ask a question
if the answer might embarrass

so we considered
slightly more of a tamper
like
I'm above your jokes
but no no no
fatal batsqueak of loser
or
I clove young joints
a boast it would be
fun to grow into
though not so much
to shrink out of

or
wIndhover you joy
transcendental but
typographically awkward

then we had it
it fitted like my skin
respectful and lifelong
a whole encyclopedia in there
map reference for a dark corner
that opens on the universe
indefinite license to represent
imaginary footnotes
so all I ever wanted

I love you jorge luis borges
and to hell with literary fashion

and you jo

on civil war

following inundation infestation invasion
measure countermeasure and scorched earth
crops officially pitiful and stores covertly emptied
here is an announcement from the ministry
let them eat roots
thank you

here is an announcement from the military
I wouldn't dig
just there
if I were you

on foreign war

birdcalls then the woods are lit
reveille

greens of spring on the way north
camouflage

turning twisting the hunters' path
outflanking

ripples across a willow pond
alert

silent village smoke rising low
reconnaissance

mountain bridges sky high
sanction

fast fast water rock crash
surge

moonshine woman washing silk
recreation

before the red leaves of autumn
victory

the eyes and hands of children
defeat

on phonetics

try not to fall
in love with the flute player
breath
try not to fall
in love with the flute player
breath

well-meant advice dear
friends though as we know
straight from that hoary classic
101 things to avoid
in the floating world

no it wasn't my intention
I knew she was trouble
but then I always liked the feel
of wisdom in my mouth
the liquids and fricatives
the stops and embouchures

try not to fall
in love with the flute player
tongue scurry
try not to fall
in love with the flute player
palate flicker
try not to fall
in love with the flute player
lip bustle

repeat love with the flute player
mimetic
repeat love with the flute player
prophetic

on nomenclature

father knew his place
it was near the north gate
of the auxiliary winter capital
in the quarter of the middling sort

I climbed it for both of us
the mountain of graduated merit
to the thud of plummeting bodies
I examined away my youth
in the hall of indelible nightmares
to the accompaniment of terminal sobbing
then it was farewell happy father

my first posting was an assistantship
in the region of windswept borders
where I gave good calligraphy
in the third war of pointless encroachment

later in the capital
I enjoyed prestigious posts
keeper of the library of unlearned lessons
and later the first curator
of the burnt library museum
yes interesting times

when I was installed on
the committee of unthinkable thoughts
under the prince with the bees in his bonnet
a new title seemed to beckon me
till all that free-form thinking
triggered the great autumn purge
resulting in five uncomfortable days

in the chamber of extruded truth
before a ceremony-free award
of the brown fan of early retirement
second class

where I live now
the locals will direct you to
the famous mountain hut
of the retired administrator
but I'm always careful to point out
it's really just my dwelling
that I've haven't got round
to calling anything fancy
and my garden is not defined
by willows or chrysanthemums
or that big mountain it clings to

what I've learned I think is
how everything under language
slips and slides and bites
and how in the end
language makes its excuses
and leaves for the beach
where every wave is new and gone

and I sit late
night rises from the valley
and one by one the lights come on
like memories and stay
wavering like memories

and later one by one go out
like names

on history

prisoner of the barbarians
for three slow years
I whiled away the winters
writing their first histories
in an ink of unspeakable origins

you may have seen copies
in the imperial library
these days probably misshelved
the book of the white tent
the book of the golden yak
the book of the grey horse-sausage

in these unlikely fruits
of my diplomacy lurks
a sweet kernel of realpolitik
that who bosses the present
is master of the past
and whoever masters the past
controls the market
for fermented mare's milk
indefinitely

could I get them to listen
to my sonorous sentences
did they stop playing
with sheep or knucklebones
even for a minute
did just one of them say
teach me to read and write
urbane and talented guest
take me to that future

for answer alas
I refer you to my later corpus
the book of the white wind
the book of the golden emptiness
the book of the grey ashes

on fruit

I drank late
with the princes
in the pavilion of green oranges

I drank late
with the hedonists
in the pavilion of low-hanging grapes

I drank late
with the courtesans
in the pavilion of ripe peaches

I drank late
with the eunuchs
in the pavilion of invisible plums

I drank late
with the sages
in the pavilion of immanent apricots

I drank late
with the plotters
in the pavilion of bitter lemons

not such a great diet
as I was shortly to discover

on lineage

big black hoodie crow
inspector of the monuments
sat upon a wall
a battlefield wall
squared up to me
eye to eye

his
black rainy night
on the clan graves
mine
blue ballad fodder

though eye to eye
might be by our days
a truce struck
an understanding shared

thinking of my folk
armed to the teeth
all sides of
the argument
blood mingled long
before it made me
in this earth

thinking of his
who flapped
and feasted here
and picked
and mixed us
impartially

on empiricism

two big woodpigeons
in stumping promenade
just came down the mound
so ideally plump
debating in their doric

a turn in the gardens
may bring no
firm conclusions
but periodically they'll
check up on the grass
to find it just
where they left it

though this is not
q e d inevitable

later I hear them
with the twilight horrors
perched in the trees and
suddenly they're hard
at those reassuring
notes to self

it's a' richt
it's a' richt davey
it's a' richt

on iconoclasm

what did you expect
these boiling-over times
a pinch of salt
a handful of shalt not
and is it safer

pound the head
till it separates
remove all trimmings
brushed glazed
moulded carved
whatever had a face and
is it what you expected
headless abattoir
rigor of lords and ladies

the furnace on the wall
that slow cooks in a pie
the devilled and the spitted
you've banked it beneath
a new white crust
out of sight but
is it any safer

blind saints still standing
the flames still
in your head

and what did you expect
and do you feel
safer

on telescopes

the man in the moon
on his high
thin platform
he's ready

almost silence
under the canopy
just that slight thrum
we call atmosphere

we're ready
so raise hands
lower eyes
lean to the position
and he falls

straight
as
light
into the bright
pool of
glass

applause

on domes

stars look down
the telescopes
at us

infinitessimal
scared of
solar winds
of being alone
of not being

but big
on headroom
on the curved space
we've filled with
calculus and yearning
and words
words words

capacious and
more oxygen for them
our prayers

good for flames too

on travel

after years
of half-seen marvels
privation yes and loss
dubious hands pointing
beyond the horizon shimmer
on the great dogshead expedition
at last we came
to the valley
of the dogsheads

they had heads like dogs'

otherwise
nothing special

okay
whatever
and other mutterings in
the expeditionary beards

they didn't take
to us either and
as we later remarked
lucky we had
those tinned supplies

and the rifles

on many

many a mickle makes a muckle

many an uncle fakes a twinkle

many a sickle nicks an ankle

many an oracle shakes a pinnacle

many a ventricle lacks a miracle

many a testicle leaks a lifecycle

many a jackal snokes a roadkill

many a jekyll sinks a psychochemical

many a theatrical overcooks a swashbuckle

many a hypothetical freaks an evangelical

many a numbskull cocks a monocle

many a heckle wrecks a versicle

many a chronicle unpacks a debacle

many a rascal hawks a sparkle

many a trachle tweaks a muscle

many a muckle maks a mickle

on bibliomancy

you yes you sir
big kilt hidden depths
just joking
yes you sir
in that dubious array
known in the cream of
woollen mills and teashops
as the ancient caledonian
am I right

you yes sir if
you'd kindly oblige me
when I turn my back
pick a page any page
from this bumper book
history of a small nation
with that elusive centrefold
of bare naked freedom

thank you now choose a date
shouldn't be hard sir
sentences are spiked with them
and next a word that leaps up
at you from the page good
and now keep them in mind

I'm ready if you are

I'm getting yes
a long knotty paragraph
bristling and slippery
not at all pleasant

in fact nightmarish considering
the nature of the bristles
the quality of the slipperiness
and now I'm getting a date
stuck deep in the paragraph
like bare feet in mud and guts
a numerical sequence
like 1920 but it's not
no a lot earlier and
the year would be 1314
am I right

thank you sir
and the word you chose
was I believe *schiltrom* yes
signifying ladies and gentlemen
a defensive prickly formation
favoured by hedgehogs
and small beleaguered nations
with little else but
long spears to sharpen

which tactic once in a while
if the badger forgets its claws
and the enemy his archers
and everybody in the battle square
stays on speaking terms
works

am I right

on healing

leaned into a farewell
brush of skins
noticing how well
her new one fitted
then it was
heigh ho off
on my big
resettlement adventure

a fresh start in
some other downtown
that was the ticket
though flaky old portico
and unswept worn steps
might be thought to mutter
end of an era

but was I downhearted
well the room had
its marks and scuffs
but not from my life
though that did turn up
later in a van
telling me gently who I was
or possibly had been

apparently the kind
who bought but
never opened
a room of one's own
a handful of dust
the end of the affair
journey to the end of the night

and my counsellors
grabbing this like big
soft-mouthed dogs said
clearly I'd been processing
much more than I'd realised
had in fact known without knowing
which could be a good sign

but best leave them
they said unopened now
and this stage of the programme
go for something new instead
think positive say yes

here we are then
fresh from the bookshop
a hundred years of solitude
by the master of magic realism

a man in front of a firing squad
remembers first seeing ice
and I've just realised
it's where I'm starting too
allowing for the magic mirror
fabulists hold up to nature

the mirror image literally
I mean I'm here with the ice
remembering the muzzle-flash

that's positive
I think
yes
cold though

on greatness

only at
his own
somewhat
double-edged
remarks

the sound
of one man
laughing

on smallness

dead
if you join in

dead if you
don't

on murder

splash in pond
make room
ancestors

ripples widen
moon and frogs resume

on suicide

almost his
last thing
that weekend

planting out bulbs
footnotes for the spring

on bread

meanwhile in the humid
bread cave glimmered
the white and the grey

grey was in father's opinion
always worth a second look
skiddy metal stairs
machine hulks and those
early morning faces
those hands in the dough
so much impure potential

grey floors also kept
just barely the lid
on his galleries
deeper than the trenches
childhood in the dark
with the pit ponies
and dusty fingerprints
on his heel of loaf
and coughing black
and never again

* * *

coal dust then
sixty years filled with
white northern early light
snowy hats and overalls
day in day out climate
of dry flour blizzards dough slush

and the fat bread flakes
that could fill a horizon

then
something
on the x-rays

that thickened
darkened
rose

fired the oven

on mysteries

fresh from the oven baked
using only the finest ingredients
although the product may contain
allegedly from time to time

    a second-hand sticking plaster
    the front end of a mouse
    a one inch flathead screw
    an untipped dog-end
    the rear end of a mouse
    a chip bag sans chips
    a bacon rind sans bacon
    a christmas cracker joke with punchline
    unfortunately

snug as a preserved debacle
in a reliquary of the patron saint
of no such thing as an accident
head-scratching as a body
uncovered in the sealed fired
dough library conundrum

but father the bakery sleuth
said as with most of life
there are only three explanations
that's two if you remember
there are no accidents

so wheel in the first suspect
please take a seat
now
when did you say
you bought this loaf
mrs wishart

on portraits

this one
ancestral
clammy
master of
the bedroom
face like
a bag of
spaniels

and her
no better than
money could buy
wattle and daub
atop a palladian
carnage

little master
rich boy
he's here too
in the birdcage
of his parrot
genes

who will grow
well-hung
about the chin
ballooning in
silk stockings
ample portrait
flesh to be

the legs carved

for heavy
perching
for the maximum
rustic
crush

eyes
to wander
the fat
rolls
of landscape
and into
secret woodland
tufts
or shady nooks
where can hide
whole villages

hands
to have and
grip hard
to set
the dogs on
you
sir

on ecstasy

          radiant eyes
the starlight
   turn to chaos

      snares of

  curious silkworm work

          those breasts
                 the apennine
                   or frost
   lily

   breath which
perfumes
            all the east

                 voice
       the hearts
music

               eclipse
         with coral lips
      the seas

   conceal no
                 face
      overcome by
            paradise

on peace

       life is
         precious dust is
  sweet disorder

    the round earth's
          ravish'd by
god
       she laughs aloud
     man of war
        who loves the skeleton

     clouded majesty and eyes
    harbingers are come see see
    lady
the lark now leaves his watery nest
    may-pole is up

    wanton troopers riding
          into the world of light

on birth

draw the curtains of
her dark entrails
and to the air
flowing
live

triumph of blue and red

joy
laughed at and forgot
thy tapers
blind
heaven

a prisoner new cast
sleeps

on the library

it shone at night
it shone beautifully

it shone like the eddystone
it shone like the fire-cave
it shone like the old torpedo works
it shone like honeycomb spreadsheets
it shone like alchemy alley
it shone like aurora midnight mass
it shone like a plainchant surge
it shone like a troubadour fragment
it shone like test-site instruments
it shone like towerblock hypodermics
it shone like a harvest moon supper
it shone like famine eyes
it shone like harmonica railtrack
it shone like the tiger sonata
it shone like chandelier futures
it shone like the twilight home past
it shone like news from another star
it shone like the road to ruin
it shone like iron in the soul
it shone like an ampoule of angel dust
it shone like a fistful of martyr clippings
it shone like oranges in a net
it shone like torches in a deep dark forest
it shone like grandma's fireside
it shone like the wicked queen's smile
it shone like the necklace left in the laurel
it shone like the ring spilled in the reeds
it shone like a god's pursuit sandals
it shone like an autumn arboretum

it shone like the cherry pond spring
it shone like a thief's deep pockets
it shone like a jackdaw's escape velocity
it shone like a pirate's night-sweats
it shone like riot in lakeside towns
it shone like an islay lock-in
it shone like a boxful of butterflies
it shone like a web at the wood's edge
it shone like blazing hilltop victory
it shone like the valley of last resort
it shone like the story of you and me

it shone all night

on afterwords

to whom
it may concern
milady
or shall I call you
cruel goddess

check
your annals
you'll see
I've never
claimed to be
first to put
these words
to use

but to be clear
my glory
is to be first
to understand them
just this way

and can I say
your glory
to receive them

can I

so
returning to
my proposition

Background Notes

on the governing of empires
Constantine VII Porphyrogennetos (*born in the purple (chamber)*)
became Emperor of Byzantium under a regency in 913, was
usurped by his grand admiral of the fleet in 920 and regained
full power in 945, reigning until 959. He was, by any standards, a
survivor, though his experiences seem to have resulted in a strong
need to write everything down. He passed down to succeeding
porphyrogennetoi a number of important compilations and
distillations, including a 53-volume encyclopaedia of statecraft,
On Governing the Empire. The 3 surviving volumes deal with the
election of emperors, embassies and (most promisingly, at least in
theory) the nature of vice and virtue. The disappearance of the other
50 volumes may be put down to a combination of carelessness,
contempt, political unrest and the fall of Constantinople in 1453.

The present author has attempted, with a change of title that
is significant, to reconstitute the missing 50 topics, though
unencumbered (scandalously) by any notion of what those topics
might originally have been. He has also played fast and loose
with time, space and a multiplicity of imperial practice, and can
only ask the indulgence of pedants and Byzantinists everywhere.

on heresy
old guidebooks of southern France plot the landscapes of dualism
and pinpoint locales favoured by the Devil, a high-profile (and
frequent) visitor. They also suggest some useful idioms.

on optics
in English, though not in German, *glasses* are so called after
the material from which the lenses used to be made. Film
of Auschwitz, only a few years further down the road than the
rampaging of Kristallnacht, shows a mound of discarded glasses,
which in the official set of accounts had a resale value. Was
not a kind of optician's chart of morality one of the great lost
Expressionist projects?

on psyche
Byzantium lives, and not only in churches, mosques and the stubs of encyclopaedias. The image of soul/mind as a subterranean reservoir with monsters is however more appropriate to the post-Freudian, post-Jungian world.

on verbs
nomads given to foreign conquest were very adept at picking up useful specialists from conquered populations. They were not however impervious to well-crafted toolboxes of "doing words" and their insidious tenses.

on forestry
impressive at first (see Francis Ponge), conifer forests soon enough exude the dismal atmosphere of resinous detritus, sensory deprivation and infinite rehash previously experienced by the author in Sunday School.

on reformation
sometimes it is precisely where religious sites have been dismantled and abandoned that we can see what is numinous in *natura naturans*.

on tragedy
Stalin, his finger on the pulse-point as usual, argued that tragedy scaled up a millionfold became merely a statistic. As for the plaster-cast businesses of hidden Paris with their haunted workshops packed with classical themes—some still featured in design magazines—we must assume that the Boss knew even less about them than he did about the masterworks of Euripides.

on bells
bells featured in trench culture in the song *The Bells of Hell Go Ting-a-Ling-a-Ling For You But Not For Me* and in the perception that there were no passing bells for those who died as cattle. But what tolls for you and me is not only confined to (*pace* John Donne) mankind.

on princesses
some furnishings catalogues seem to channel the House of Windsor, but really this is a global discussion.

on fire
the regular charring of the slopes of the Croatian littoral has been attributed to a shortage of underbrush-clearing goats. Consequently, goats are seldom listed among the casualties.

on stars
of course, much of this is no more than an illusion.

on statues
though Stalin has largely left the plinth, Russian cities maintain their statues of Lenin, characteristically pointing somewhere or other. Sometimes he was pointing quite far out of town.

on ballads
happy families resemble each other, but unhappy families are prime ballad fodder. Many readers nowadays prefer to take their ballads in fragments, with a good malt whisky.

on midlife
a middle-aged man can recognise his predicament anywhere, even (or rather particularly) in his wife's magazine collection.

on taxonomy
classification is a specifically human activity, like using opposable thumbs in ways detrimental to the rest of creation.

on protocol
as Shakespeare and the Borgias taught us, a sense of what was fitting was not always, in Renaissance courts, extended to health and safety issues. The food-taster's position was at once exalted and hapless, and seldom hereditary.

on leadership
a simple guided country walk may, infiltrated by the very values the walk is ostensibly escaping, become a real struggle for mastery.

on palaces
one might ask, where is *The House of Mirth*? Or even *The House of Fun*? But this looks like ancient Thebes. Enough said.

on monasteries
any decent guide to the seashore will afford a flash of the monkish lives lived on those margins.

on bedlam
while the public took their guided tours of the noisome precincts of the Bethlehem Hospital, seriously bewigged lepidopterists were settling down to give the moth population of these islands an assortment of freak-show names.

on memory
tying Arthurian legend to the evidential sobriety of archaeological reports has never been easy. On a personal note, remembering things seems increasingly a problem too.

on the senses
Breton saints can get very small indeed, sometimes even too small for burial or for any physical reality beyond that of the unique painted statue in a parish church. This seems at once satisfying and, in its comfortable local way, heretical.

on salvage
Borges would never have had a tattoo, but might have savoured the phrase *pushing ink.*

on civil war
digging for victory is a less viable measure in these circumstances.

on foreign war
conflict and its aftermath are threaded in and out of the classical poetry of the Far East. Western military vocabulary is usually brief and to the point, yet ultimately evasive.

on phonetics
the floating world describes the hedonistic urban culture of ancient Edo and other Japanese cities. The soundtrack was interesting.

on nomenclature
Chinese civil service exams in the Imperial centuries were gruelling, but successful candidates learned that life could be made bearable and even interesting through tireless labelling.

on history
no-one who has travelled to Mongolia, one possible setting for this poem, could forget the boiled horse sausage.

on fruit
the problem of what to do in the evenings had, at some stage or other, to be confronted by court officials. The alternative was at best dissolution and ill-health, at worst many flavours of mischief.

on lineage
Culloden is a case in point; the author's ancestors in the Argyll Militia, behind a stone wall, fired from a right angle on other ancestors charging with the Highland clans towards other ancestors in the Government ranks. Crows moved in just in time to feature in the laments.

on empiricism
several former pupils or masters of the Royal High School in Edinburgh have written poems in which pigeons make an appearance. The birds' resemblance to portly philosophers of the Scottish Enlightenment (a little forgetful of tailors' appointments) has however been missed hitherto.

on iconoclasm
how angry is God? Does He visit hard times on us because of an objection to figural art in holy spaces? What, actually, is being cooked up here (see also *on reformation*)?

on telescopes/on domes
sober descriptions of the sky at night are easily infiltrated by the music of the spheres and a certain consequent sadness.

on travel
the arrival of a band of travel-stained beardies would have understandably disconcerted the dogsheads, an ancient race of whom these were to be, it appears, the last remnants.

on many
however pithy the maxim, *muckle* and *mickle* mean, in different Scottish dialect areas, the very same thing. George Washington, from a north-east English family, wrote "many a pickle makes a mickle". The other Scots words incorporated here (*snoke*, to sniff around, *trachle*, a wearying task, *jekyll*, a medical man lacking full mastery of experimental methods), are eloquent of several aspects of Scottish life.

on bibliomancy
the patter of the stage illusionist is always nervier in urban Scottish venues. The *schiltrom,* a low-budget defensive formation turned to brilliant offensive use at Bannockburn (1314), went out of fashion in early Renaissance military circles, though spectacular defeat interspersed with the occasional surprise victory remained the pattern of Scottish arms.

on healing
the Céline was never in fact opened, on ideological grounds, but García Márquez remained a great comfort with *Love in the Time of Cholera* and *Chronicle of a Death Foretold.*

on greatness/ on smallness
Stalin's habit of amusing himself with his own one-liners, against a background of nervous titters, is archetypical bully-boy behaviour. Humour can indeed be a suspect package when times are uncertain. Those driving the French Revolution set citizens a severe test when they named one of the days of the month of Brumaire, in the new calendar, *Fig.*

on murder/ on suicide
the smaller the form, the shorter the fuse. Haiku enthusiasts will hardly give credit for the regulation 17 syllables here (itself a contentious requirement), such will be their distaste for the 5-line split form and the use of rhyme. We should certainly be prepared for future conflagrations in the ranks of monochordists, champions of the single-line poem.

on bread
the author's father went down a coal mine to work at the age of 12. This was during WWI; four of the child miner's uncles died on the Western Front. Later he became a master baker and confectioner; the cake in his window modelled on the Floral Clock in Princes Street Gardens—featuring a march past of toy soldiers synchronised with the one o'clock gun fired from Edinburgh Castle across the road—was a perennial Festival favourite.

on mysteries
the author's father used to regale him with stories of such outrages. Memory tends to blend them now with episodes of the first TV series of *Maigret*. The preference was that the customer would crumble and confess everything, but employee spite was often a fruitful second line of enquiry. For several years, though more likely for Oedipal reasons, the author would eat no bread.

on portraits
shamefully, several National Trust publications were damaged in the making of this poem.

on ecstasy/ on peace/ on birth
the achievement of a poetic age, for example the first half of the English seventeenth century, can be deduced from a trawl through its minor poets and indexes of first lines.

on the library
the McDonald Road Library in Edinburgh sparked many a bookish life and many a library career too, grounded in the awareness that behind every beacon of knowledge is a sound overdue fines system.

on afterwords
the troubadour era took poetics to new and shameless levels of manipulation. *Amour lointain?* Believe it if you like.

www.ingramcontent.com/pod-product-compliance
Lightning Source LLC
Chambersburg PA
CBHW031930080426
42734CB00007B/625